TRAVEL & TRANSPORT

BY ROBIN TWIDDY

BookLife PUBLISHING

©2019
BookLife Publishing Ltd.
King's Lynn
Norfolk PE30 4LS
All rights reserved.
Printed in Malaysia.

A catalogue record for this book is available from the British Library.

ISBN: 9781-78637-628-2

Written by:
Robin Twiddy

Edited by:
Madeline Tyler

Designed by:
Gareth Liddington

Photocredits: All images are courtesy of Shutterstock.com.

Cover – Lilia Beck, connel, Fasttailwind, donatas1205, 2 – muratart, 4 – Joseph Sohm, Crafter, 5 – Arcansel, Swapan Photography, 6 – Twinsterphoto, Don Mammoser, 7 – Postrach, Smithsonian Institution, 8 – Karasev Victor, vladimir salman, 9 – Lisa F. Young, AzmanMD, 10 – John T. Daniels, Andrey_Kuzmin, Pecold, 11 – Ivan Cholakov, Ryan Fletcher, 12 – Vander Wolf Images, Ivan Cholakov, 13 – Suksin, Fer Gregory, Sergiy Kuzmin, 14 - Nicole Patience, 15 - Andy Dingley, Chakrit Yenti, Regisser, 16 - Denis Belitsky, nha.library, 17 - Fouad A. Saad, Xseon, Samuel J. Hodson, 18 - Alvov, dikobraziy, 19 - seabreezesky, Mpftmead, Bakalusha, 20 - art_photo_sib, E-Pics Bildarchiv, 21 - JoJan, PD-USGOV, 22 - Astronaut David R. Scott, 23 - NASA/Bill Ingalls, Jason and Bonnie Grower, 24 - Andrey Armyagov, USAF, SAHACHATZ, 25 - adike, Rawpixel.com, 26 - Tyler Olson, sebra, 27 - Dima Sidelnikov, weedezign, 28 - betto rodrigues, Leonel Calara, 29 - Rickman21, Kite_rin, 30 - metamorworks.

Images are courtesy of Shutterstock.com. With thanks to Getty Images, Thinkstock Photo and iStockphoto.

All facts, statistics, web addresses and URLs in this book were verified as valid and accurate at time of writing.
No responsibility for any changes to external websites or references can be accepted by either the author or publisher.

CONTENTS

Words that look like <u>this</u> are explained in the glossary on page 31.

HOW CAN MACHINES CHANGE THE WORLD?

When a ship called the Mayflower sailed from England to America in 1620, the journey was not easy, and it was not short. The 102 passengers on board wanted to start a new life in America, but it took them 66 days to cross the Atlantic Ocean. Today that same journey would take less than eight hours. Travel today is much quicker and, just as importantly, it is safer.

TO TRAVEL OR NOT TO TRAVEL

From simple machines to complex inventions, technology and machinery can solve problems, make life easier, and change society. Understanding the everyday machines we take for granted can help us understand the world around us a little better. One big problem that people have had to face is travel: how to do it quickly but also safely.

Why do we invent new things? We invent new machines to solve problems! And of course, when a new machine solves a big problem, then it has the potential to change the world. The machines that revolutionised transport and travel made the world feel smaller and connected people more than any other invention before the internet.

In many areas, machines are changed and invented to do other things. Did you know that the pacemaker was originally invented to just measure heart rates, but Wilson Greatbatch, the pacemaker's inventor, used the wrong part and made something new? Inventions like these can lead to huge changes in society.

Pacemaker

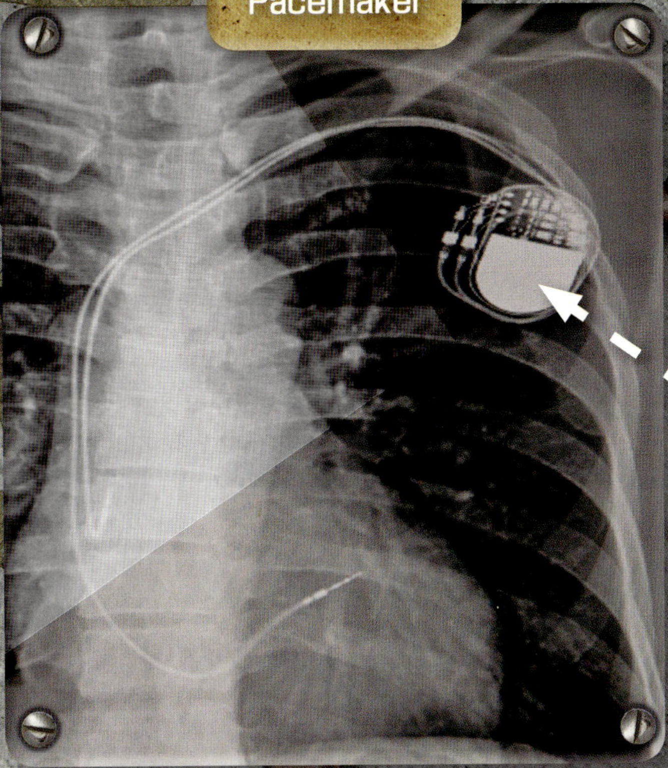

A HAPPY ACCIDENT!

HORSEPOWER

THE OPEN ROAD TO POSSIBILITY

We have come a long way from the horse-drawn carriages of our ancestors. The automobile, or car as we call it, has changed how we travel and made travel much easier than it was before. We don't think twice about hopping into the car to visit somewhere exciting 80 kilometres (km) away.

China produces more cars than any other country in the world.

CAR VS HORSE

If you wanted to travel 80 km to visit family or for a nice day out 200 years ago, your journey would take 8–12 hours in a horse and cart! Making that same journey in a car would take around one hour. Wow, that is a lot of time saved!

TRAVEL TRUTHS

In 1900 there were 25,000 cars in the world. Today there are over one billion!

CARS – THE BEGINNING

Believe it or not, in the earliest days of cars, petrol cars were not the only option. In the early 20th century, 40 percent (%) of American cars were steam-powered, 38 % were powered by electricity, and the other 22 % were petrol-powered.

ELECTRIC CARS IN THE 1800s?

As early as 1830, inventors were experimenting with the idea of an electric car, but it wasn't until the 1880s that various inventors started making practical electric cars. To begin with, electric cars looked promising, so what happened? Why did petrol become the most common available type of power for cars?

This is an early electric car in 1910.

WHY PETROL?

Although the early electric car was very popular, there was a very serious problem with it. Very few towns or villages had electricity at this time. This meant that it was very difficult to recharge the batteries that they ran on. But what really killed the electric car was Henry Ford's Model T. The Model T cost $650 while the electric roadster cost $1,750.

Ford Model T

Henry Ford changed the way people manufactured cars, with the introduction of the production line. This was a method of making cars where, instead of the engineers moving all their tools from one car to another, the cars would move along a conveyor belt to the engineer.

Even today, most factories use the methods developed by Ford for efficient manufacturing.

WHAT HAS THE CAR CHANGED?

Cars changed the face of almost every country. Suburban areas and cities have been designed and redesigned with the car in mind, and roads have been cut into landscapes that stood untouched for thousands of years. For many people, learning to drive is a rite of passage, much like leaving school or getting your first job.

For better or worse, the success of the car led to an increase in the value and use of crude oil to make fuel for cars, creating a whole new industry. The car also gave people the freedom to relocate. Travelling across the country to start a new life wasn't nearly as scary as it had been before.

Offshore Drilling Rig

TRAVEL TRUTHS

The average car has around 30,000 parts!

IS IT A BIRD? IS IT A...?

In 1903, two brothers from Ohio changed the world forever. Orville and Wilbur Wright successfully flew the first powered and manned aircraft on the 17th of December, 1903. And with that unsteady 12-second flight, a new age of aviation was born.

The Wright Flyer

ACROSS THE BAY

Those clever Wright brothers weren't the only ones working on the problem of flight, but they were the first to crack it. Only 11 years later, Tony Jannus became the first commercial pilot, flying passengers across Tampa Bay, Florida.

TRAVEL TIMES

DEP: St. Petersburg (Florida)
ARR: Tampa

By Steamboat: 2 Hours
By Train: 4 – 12 Hours
By Car: 20 Hours
By Plane: About 20 Minutes

SCIENCE IN THE SKY

Today, planes come in all sorts of shapes and sizes, from large airliners to small fighter jets, but it is the same science that keeps them in the air. The clever shape of a plane's wings changes the air pressure above and below it. This change in air pressure gives the plane lift.

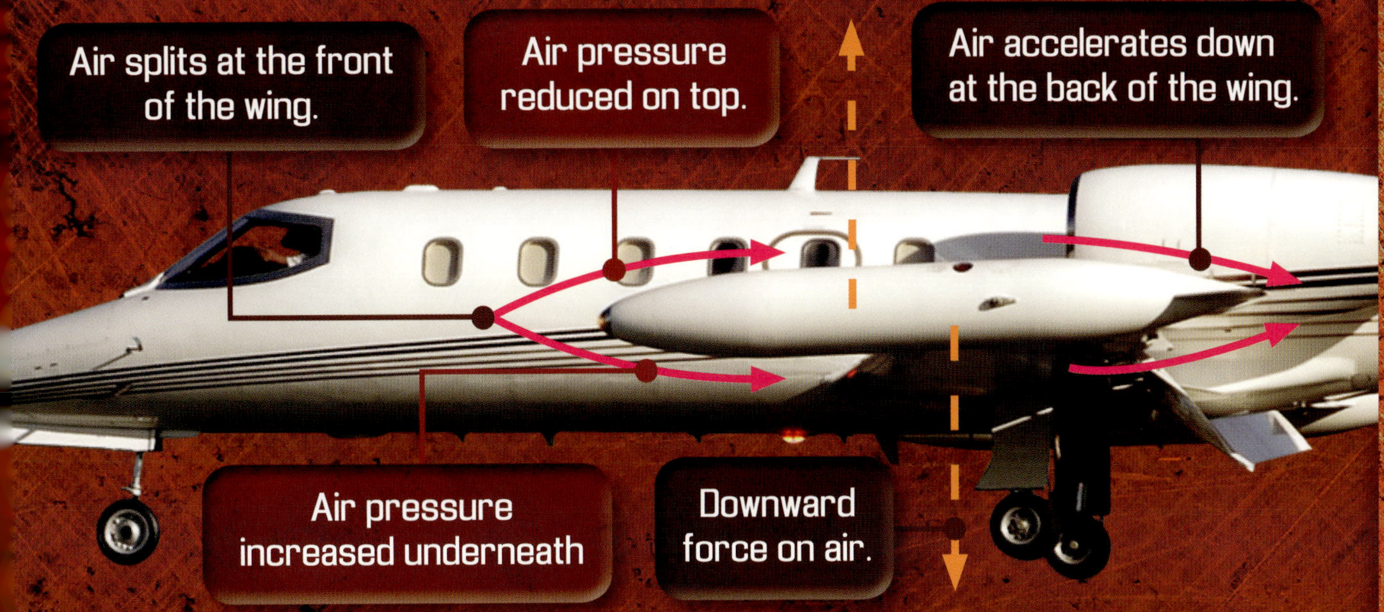

The plane's engine pushes it forward but the shape of the wing forces air down and the plane up, giving it lift.

Since the Wright brothers' first flight, the aeroplane has been constantly updated and refined. The field of aeronautics – the study of how air moves around objects such as planes – has helped engineers to make planes faster, safer and easier to fly.

BY AIR

A WHOLE NEW WORLD

For thousands of years, people have wished to be able to fly like birds and, thanks to the Wright brothers, they finally can. However, the invention of the aeroplane has done more than just allow people to fly: it has changed what we eat, how we travel and how we fight wars.

The Red Arrows

WAR IN THE AIR

The invention of the aeroplane changed war forever. The results of this were most dramatically seen in the Second World War, where both sides used aeroplanes to deliver aerial attacks, dropping both parachute troops (paratroopers) and bombs.

BRINGING PEOPLE TOGETHER

As well as changing how wars are fought, aeroplanes have also helped to bring us together. Thanks to the aeroplane, there is nowhere on Earth that is too remote to reach. The invention of the aeroplane also meant that food could be transported long distances without rotting or going off.

HOW ELSE HAVE AEROPLANES CHANGED THE WORLD?

TRAVEL TRUTHS

You are 19 times safer travelling by plane than you are by car.

Aeroplanes have not just made transport easier, quicker and safer, but they have also had a wider impact on the world of technology. Innovations in technology to help with travel have pushed lots of other inventions forward. Here are a couple of things that we can thank aeroplanes for...

Spacecraft have taken us to the moon – and beyond!

Microwave

This invention was based on technology used in radar to detect aeroplanes.

BY RAIL

The Industrial Revolution changed everything, from how we work to how we play. There was one piece of technology that we really associate with the success of the Industrial Revolution, and that was the train and rail system. Today we use trains to travel long and short distances, across the country or to get about the city.

TRACK FACTS

US:
250,000 km of rail track

China:
100,000 km of rail track

Russia:
85,000 km of rail track

UK:
30,000 km of rail track

IT ALL BEGAN WITH STEAM

Although most trains that we see today are powered by diesel or electricity, or sometimes both, in the early days they were all powered by steam. As we have already seen, the steam engine was used in some early cars, but it was its use in locomotives that really changed the world.

I DREAM OF STEAM

The steam engine was first invented to pump water out of flooded mines in Spain in 1606. Over the next 100 years, many inventors worked on improving the steam engine. In 1775, inventor James Watt and manufacturer Matthew Boulton transformed a steam-powered pump into something that could power almost any type of machine. This gave birth to the age of steam.

LAYING THE TRACKS TO THE FUTURE

In 1804, a man called Richard Trevithick put the first steam engine on tracks. He used it to pull nearly 10 tons of iron and 70 men along almost 15 km of track across Britain. It moved at a slow but steady 8 kilometres per hour (kph). In 1830, the first regular passenger train went into service and 15 years later the country was covered in a web of railway tracks that changed Britain's landscape and people forever.

National Railway Museum, York

HOW DID TRAINS CHANGE THE TIME?

In Britain, there is a standard time that everyone follows. This is called Greenwich Mean Time (GMT). However, people haven't always used GMT. Every town used to keep their own time – for example, Bristol was 10 minutes behind GMT. This caused a lot of confusion and meant that passengers would have to reset their watches as they passed each station. In 1852, Bristol changed their time to be the same as GMT. Over the following three years, the rest of the towns in Britain began using GMT too.

THE LIFE BLOOD OF ENGLAND

The railway system became like the veins in a body; it connected all the important parts of Britain and transported important materials and goods, delivering them all over the country. The rail system gave people the ability to travel safely and at speed; businesses could move raw materials from mines or harbours at one end of the country to factories at the other end with ease.

Modern trains run on electricity, not steam.

A colourised photograph taken at Teignmouth, England between 1890 and 1900.

REINVENTING THE HOLIDAY

Until the rail system and the steam train, holidays were only for the rich, and most people could not get away from home often, if at all. With rail lines connecting small towns, cities and coastal towns, working people could, for the first time, travel to the coast and stay there on holiday.

HOW DOES IT WORK?

Steam engines work by burning a fossil fuel called coal to heat water, which then produces steam. The steam moves a piston that turns the cogs and wheels of the train. Although the steam engine was an amazing invention that changed the world, it was not very good for the environment.

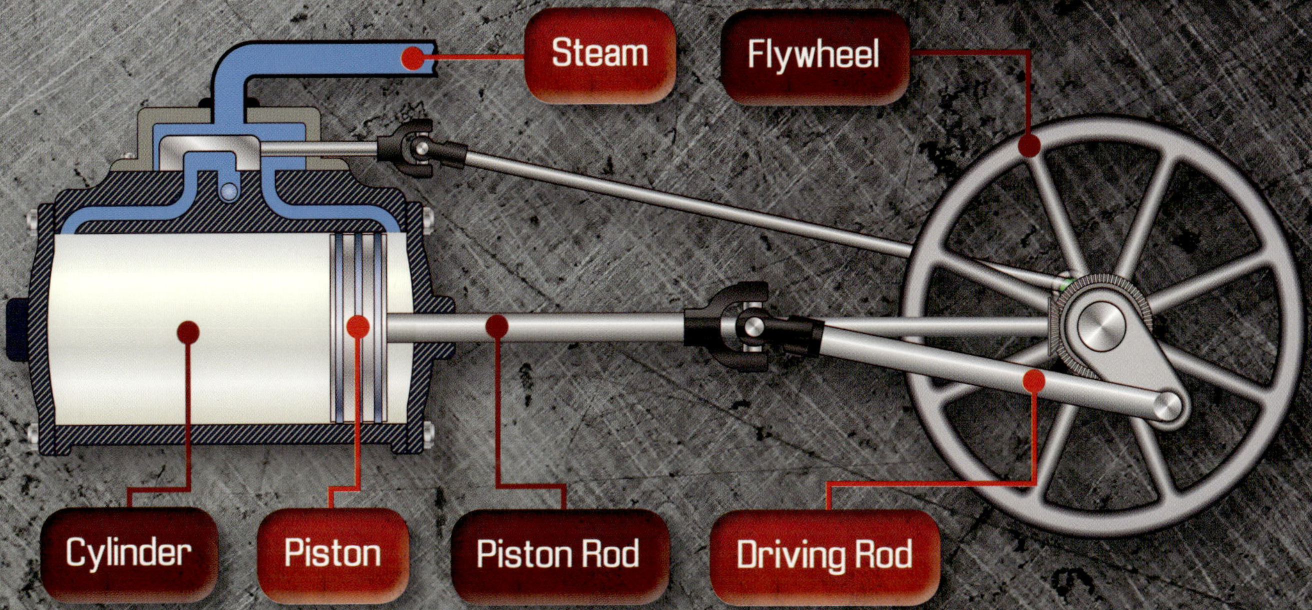

FROM STEAM TO CLEAN

The transition from the dirty coal-powered steam train to the modern electric train began in Germany in 1879. It soon reached the US and the UK as their need to replace the soot-spewing trains in the underground systems increased.

BY SEA

STEAMING AHEAD

At the same time that steam power was revolutionising the factories and establishing the rail system, inventors were trying to use that same power to cross the oceans. Until the first steam-powered ships, travelling across the ocean was dangerous and difficult and, most of all, relied on the wind.

Sailing Ship

STEAM-POWERED TRADE

The invention of the steamship, or steamer, had a huge effect on global trade. Not only was the steamship free from relying on the wind being in the right direction, but it proved to be a faster way to travel. It wasn't long before steamships became more popular than sailing ships.

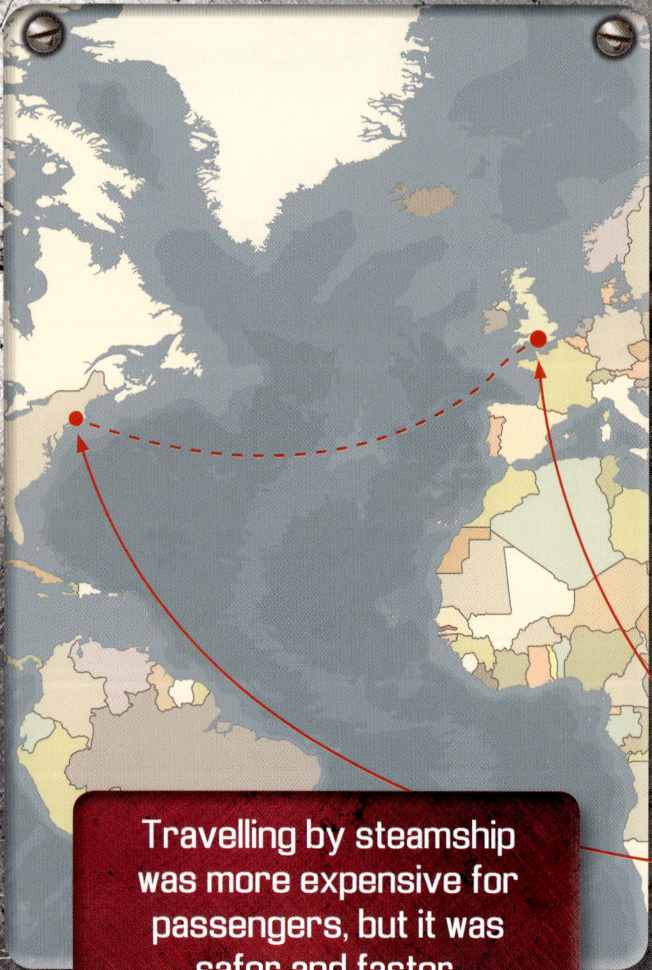

Travelling by steamship was more expensive for passengers, but it was safer and faster.

TRAVEL TIMES

DEP: Portsmouth, UK
ARR: Rhode Island, US

By Sailing Ship: 6-12 weeks
By Steamship: 2 weeks

NO MORE STEAM

Just like the car, the steamship would eventually be replaced by ships powered by diesel and electricity. Modern tankers, cruise ships and trawlers all run on diesel or electricity now. By around 1910, most ships were starting to be built with diesel engines.

Around 20% of a cruise ship is taken up by the engines and other essential equipment.

The SS United States is an ocean liner – a type of ship built for speed. She holds the record for the fastest ocean liner ever built, crossing the Atlantic Ocean in 3 days and 12 hours at a speed of around 54 kph. By the end of the 1960s, travelling by passenger plane had become more affordable and was, of course, much quicker than travelling by boat. This meant that many people began travelling by plane instead of by boat.

The SS United States

The SS United States is 301 metres long. It is 30 metres longer than the Titanic. The ship was designed to be fireproof and was built without using any wood with one exception; the ship's grand pianos, which were made from fire-resistant wood.

THE MYSTERY BELOW

Human beings have devoted a lot of time and energy to exploring our planet. As we have already seen, incredible machines have been built to help us explore the land and skies, and even cross whole oceans. But, for a long time, the world below the ocean's surface was a mystery.

Early Diving Suit

Bathysphere

THE BOLD AND THE BRAVE

In 1930, two men went where no humans had been before – William Beebe and Otis Barton travelled to the deep sea in their steel bathysphere. The bathysphere was a hollow steel ball less than one and a half metres across. It had two tanks that fed oxygen in and was connected to a ship on the surface by a steel cable.

The Aqua-Lung was the first diving equipment that regulated air flow, allowing divers to go deeper than ever before.

THE AQUA-LUNG

As far back as the 1700s, people have been designing and building diving suits, but none of these allowed the diver to move freely or explore very deep water. However, in 1943, Jacques-Yves Cousteau and Émile Gagnan perfected the Aqua-Lung. The Aqua-Lung was the first self-contained underwater breathing apparatus (scuba) and led to the development of the modern scuba gear we know today.

MAPPING THE SEA

Sonar is an acronym for sound, navigation and ranging. It was invented during the Second World War to spot submarines. It uses sound to map underwater landscapes. Sonar has made navigating the seas both above and below the surface much safer and easier.

Submarines use sonar to navigate the inky-black depths of the oceans.

INTO SPACE!

THE FINAL FRONTIER

It takes a brave person to dive into the ocean in a metal ball. In fact, there is only one place that is more dangerous than the depths of the ocean: outer space... Because the journey is as dangerous as the destination, we need some pretty amazing machines to get us there.

IT'S NOT ROCKET SCIENCE... OH WAIT

The first and most important machine that we can thank for getting us into space is the rocket. During the 1960s, the US and the Soviet Union were in a race to see who could get into space first. Both sides had scientists working for them who had worked on military rockets during the Second World War.

The moon landing would not have been possible without those scientists and their rockets.

RISK, REWARD AND ROCKETS!

Now we use computers to run simulations before launching a rocket into space. However, the computers of the 1960s were not powerful enough to do this, so there was a lot more risk then. A lot of force is necessary to overpower Earth's gravity. This force is provided by the rockets. Think about them as a controlled explosion.

WHAT IS HAPPENING INSIDE A ROCKET DURING TAKE-OFF?

Rockets need thrust to take off and to overcome Earth's gravity. Thrust is the force that pushes the rocket up. The thrust is created by burning fuel. Rockets carry a lot of fuel that burns slowly – when the fuel burns, it produces gas that escapes at the bottom of the rocket. It is this escaping gas that creates thrust.

Rockets used for take-off are actually a series of rockets that work together. When one uses all its fuel it breaks apart and falls away making the whole thing lighter. The remaining rockets then have less weight to push.

GPS

WHAT IS GPS?

GPS is short for Global Positioning System. It is a satellite navigation system used to locate the position of things on Earth. It was developed by the US military but is now available to everyone. Phones, cars, planes, ships and all sorts of other devices and companies use GPS now.

A satellite is something that orbits another object.

HOW DOES GPS WORK?

The GPS system uses 24 satellites all around the globe. They move around the Earth at an incredible speed of 11,000 kph. The satellites are spread out; this means that there are always four that can see any part of the Earth at any time. These satellites send a signal down with the exact time and the position of the satellite.

TRIANGULATION

So how does this information help you travel? A GPS receiver, such as the one in your phone or a car, works out where it is on Earth based on how far away it is from each satellite. This is called triangulation. If your GPS receiver can catch the signals of three satellites, it can work out where you are.

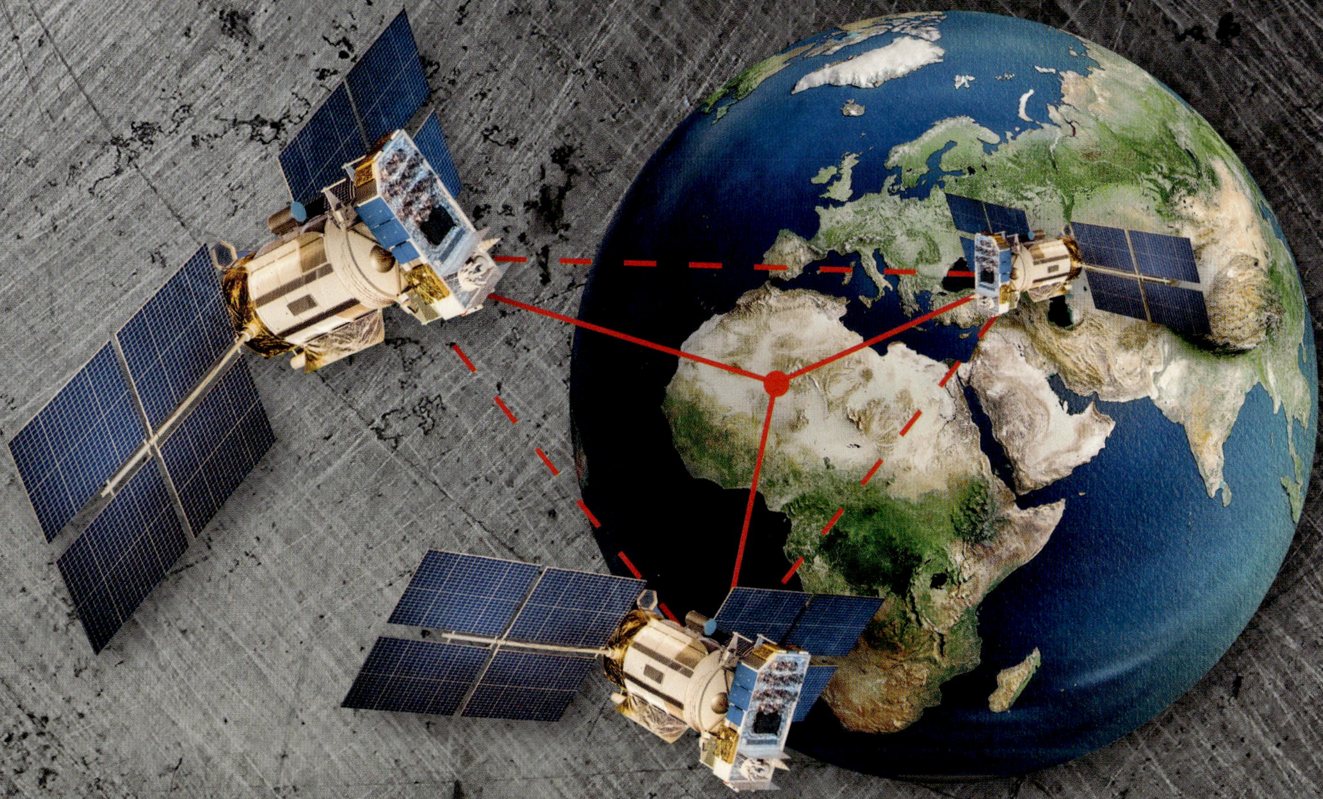

With GPS to help us, it is much harder to get lost!

WHAT HAS GPS DONE FOR US?

GPS has made a really big difference in the world. It has made travelling safer, customers and companies can keep track of packages being transported, the police can use it to track stolen things, it can even help you find your lost phone. We have the rocket to thank for putting all those satellites into orbit around the Earth and giving us GPS.

COMPUTERS

COMPUTER SAYS GO

If there is one machine that has changed the world as much as the wheel did thousands of years ago, it must be the computer. Whether it is a desktop computer at home, a tablet computer, the phone in your pocket or a huge bank of servers, these clever machines have had a huge impact on our lives. So, how have computers and the internet changed how we travel?

PLANNING A TRIP

Planning a trip has never been as easy as it is now. Before you even get to your destination, you can use the internet to investigate all the available activities – maybe you want to visit a theme park? You can find out what time it opens, how to find it, what other people thought of it, it and how to pay for your tickets. You can find the answers to all of these questions before you've even left the house.

COMPARE THE MARKET

Before computers, if you wanted to get the best price for your holiday, you would have to visit several high-street travel agents, spend time getting the information you needed from each one, and compare the different deals yourself. This takes a lot of time and effort. With the internet at your fingertips, you can compare lots of deals quickly and easily, and all in one place – meaning you can get a great deal without even having to leave the house!

Would you rather go to a travel agent or use the internet to book a trip?

ARE YOU LOST?

What do you do if you are lost? Do you use a compass and the stars to find your way? Maybe you have a paper map – you will need to find a landmark nearby to work out where you are on it. You probably use the map on a phone or a tablet. Remember those satellites? Your phone will use them to show you exactly where you are with GPS and where you need to go. Wow!

Do you have any games that use GPS? Maybe when you take photos, it lists your location; that's GPS at work!

VIRTUAL TRAVEL

WHAT DOES IT MEAN?

Reality is the actual world around us, but virtual reality (VR) is a world we can experience that is created by a computer, just like a level in your favourite computer game. A virtual world could be a very close copy of a real place or somewhere completely made up.

VR has been around since the late 1980s, but it wasn't very good then.

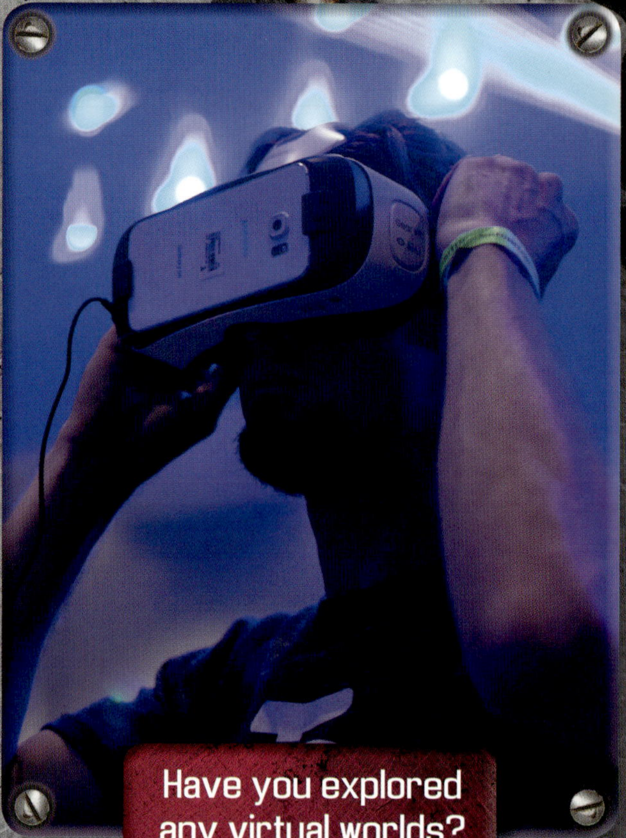

Have you explored any virtual worlds?

By using 360-degree cameras to capture the real world, people can make nearly exact VR copies to explore.

VIRTUAL REALITY MACHINES

For virtual reality to work, you need a very powerful computer and a virtual reality (VR) headset. When we put on a VR headset it tricks our eyes and minds into thinking we are really somewhere else. When you move your head to look around, the image moves too. This is what makes us feel like we are in the virtual world.

VIRTUAL APPLICATIONS

So, how has VR changed travel? Thanks to VR, people who can't travel for one reason or another can now visit distant places virtually. Some holiday resorts now give you the chance to take a VR tour of their hotel and resort. This means that you can get a feeling of what it is like to stay there.

VIRTUAL TIME TRAVEL

Most scientists believe that time travel is impossible, but VR may have given us a way. Some companies have been making historical VR experiences that let us see what it was like to live in and explore places from the distant past. You could see a Roman centurion preparing for war or a Norman castle in all its glory.

THE TRAVEL OF TOMORROW

SMART LUGGAGE

Can you imagine never having to carry your luggage again? Well if Smart Luggage becomes a reality you won't have to. It will follow you faithfully like a pet dog to your location.

DRIVERLESS CARS

Soon cars might drive themselves! Driverless cars are vehicles that do not need a human for them to drive safely. They use sensors to see, and computer software to make decisions. Driverless cars can make decisions quicker than humans, but do you think they will make the right decisions?

HOVERBOARDS

How cool would it be to have a skateboard that hovers? Well, it turns out a lot of engineers think it would be cool too. There are a lot of engineers working on floating boards using magnets, fans and thrust, like a rocket. But it looks like a working hoverboard is still a long way off.

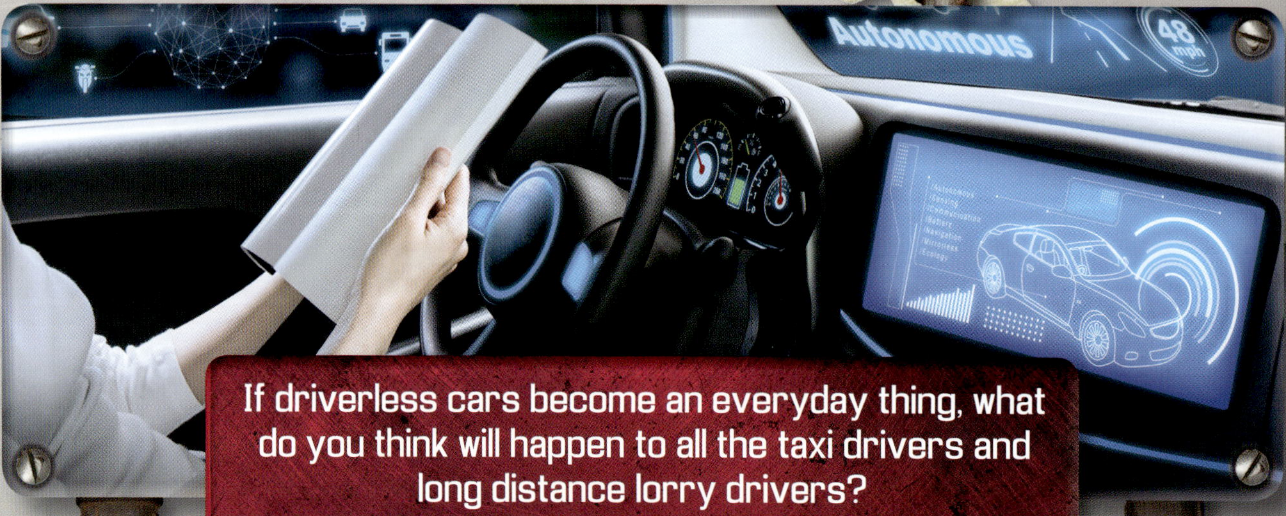

If driverless cars become an everyday thing, what do you think will happen to all the taxi drivers and long distance lorry drivers?

GLOSSARY

acronym	a word made using the first letter or letters of several other words
aerial	to do with activity in the air
ancestors	people from whom one is descended, for example a great-grandparent
aviation	the science, act or practice of flying aeroplanes
commercial	having to do with trade, business and making money
efficient	getting the most out of something in the best way possible
fossil fuel	fuel, such as coal, oil and gas, that formed millions of years ago from the remains of animals and plants
gravity	the force that pulls everything downwards towards the centre of the Earth
harbours	sheltered areas of water where boats can be anchored
Industrial Revolution	a period of time from the late 1700s to the early 1800s when technology changed how things were made
innovations	inventions or methods that do things in a new way
locomotives	powered railway vehicles
manufactured	made in large quantities
manufacturer	a company that makes large quantities of something
military	a country's army and things that relate to it
orbits	to travel in a circular or almost-circular path around an object in space, influenced by gravity
pacemaker	a device that helps keep a regular heartbeat
piston	a short cylinder closely fitted inside a tube that is moved by pressure
potential	possible of or capable of coming into being
pressure	a continuous physical force exerted on an object, which is caused by something pressing against it
refined	something that has been made more pure by removing materials or substances from it
regulated	controlled and maintained
remote	controlled from a distance
revolutionised	when something has been changed to a large degree
rite of passage	important events in a person's life
sensors	electronic devices that monitor something and react to changes
servers	computers and programs that are dedicated to maintaining and managing a network of other computers
simulations	computer-generated representations of reality
society	a collection of people living together
software	computer programs
suburban	of or to do with communities near to cities
travel agents	people who help you to plan and book travel arrangements

INDEX